LET'S WRITE A STORY

Eddie Jones (Daddy J),
staring George and Selma

Published by American Publishing
ISBN: 978-1-965649-16-9

How do you make up a story? First, something exciting must happen! Stories are fun when something big or tricky shows up. Some of the best stories begin when someone faces change, danger, or a challenge.

Let's see what danger looks like in a story. You have a happy dog. He likes to nap in the sun.

But today, while he's sleeping, a squirrel dashes past and—zoom!—your dog runs out the door and chases it into the street!

Now something is happening. That's the start of a story. Next we need a hero!

Every story needs: A Boy or Girl (pretend you are this person). A Big Want ("But, Mommy, I NEED this bike to catch our dog!"). A Problem (something or someone gets in the way—shop closed). A Fun Journey (your boy or girl goes on an adventure).

We read stories because we want to see what happens. We smile when the boy or girl is brave. We worry when they're in danger. We cheer when they keep going. We feel happy when they find what they need—or sad when they don't.

Make your own story! Ask these questions: Who is the boy or girl? What do they really want? What makes it hard? What do they do next?

That's how you start a story and begin to build it. Everything that happens should connect to what happened before or what's coming next.

We read stories because we care about the boy or girl in the story. We tag along because we want to go on the journey with them!

What is the worst thing that has happened to you this week? That could be the start of a story.

EXAMPLE OF
PLOT IN ACTION

Inspired by The Parable of the Prodigal Son:
Luke 15:11–32

Act One Introduction: One morning, after Selma reminded George for the second time to put his plate in the sink, she added, "Remember, George, we have to pick up after ourselves."

Inciting Incident / Great Disturbance: George crossed his arms and said, "No! I'm NOT going to pick up."

Call to Action: "I'm going to Grandmama's!" George said.

Identification of Your Lead's Goal: "She lets me do anything I want and I want to do what I want."

Lead Character Advances Toward His Goal: He stuffed pretzels in his pockets, grabbed a cookie, and marched out the door in his socks.

Act Two Fun & Games: At first, George loved being at Grandmama's. She let him eat chocolate kisses after a snack. When he refused to pick up his toys, she picked them up. They watched cartoons until way past lunchtime. George told Grandmama's kitty, "Selma can't boss me around. Neither can Grandmama. I'm the boss now!"

Small Hurdles: But soon, things started to change. Grandmama smiled less. She turned off the TV in the middle of *Cars on Patrol*. When he cried "NO!" she didn't make him feel better with a hug.

Status Change: Then Grandmama said, "No cookie until you eat your carrots. No *Cars on Patrol* until you pick up your toys.

And no more chocolate candy. Sweets make your teeth rot."

Large Hurdles, Death, Danger, & Conflict: While pouting, his tummy began to hurt. "Too many cheese crackers," Grandmama said. His socks were wet from walking outside without shoes. Worst of all, Grandmama washed his favorite blanket... and it was still in the dryer.

Black Moment: He whispered to Kitty, "Grandmama has rules, too. More than at Selma's. But now I'm stuck."

Glimmer of Hope: When Grandmama asked if George wanted her to walk him back to Selma's house, he replied, "Would you?"

Act Three Transition: When he reached the edge of the yard, Selma yelled, "George?"

Walk to the Cross: Selma scowled. "What are you doing back here?"

Win or Lose: "I missed you."

Climax: "I missed you, too, but rules are rules."

"I know. I'm sorry."

"It's okay. You're just in time. We just finished baking cookies. Want one?"

Tie up loose ends: That evening, Selma and George laughed so hard while playing Frank and Clara that milk came out of his nose. He picked up toys without being asked. He turned off the TV after one episode of *Cars on Patrol*. And when it was time to go to bed, he didn't cry—even though his blanket was still at Grandmama's. He had Sweet Selma to read him a book, and that was enough.

www.ingramcontent.com/pod-product-compliance
Lightning Source LLC
Chambersburg PA
CBHW040850120626
46547CB00001B/101